A PAPER ARK

A Paper Ark

ANNA ADAMS

PETERLOO POETS

First published in 1996
by Peterloo Poets
2 Kelly Gardens, Calstock, Cornwall PL18 9SA, U.K.

A catalogue record for this book is available
from the British Library

ISBN 1-871471-62-1

Printed in Great Britain by
Latimer Trend & Company Ltd, Plymouth

for Meenakshi and Anjana

ACKNOWLEDGEMENTS are due to the editors of the following journals: *Acumen, Country Life, Encounter, Orbis, Pennine Platform, Poetry Canada, Poetry Durham, Poetry Matters, PN Review, Poetry Review, Spectator, Staple, The Countryman, Western Mail* (as a winner of the Cardiff Lit. Fest. competition in 1987), and *Yorkshire Journal*.

Several of the poems were included in the pamphlets: *Brother Fox* (Midnag, 1983), *Six Legs Good* (Mandeville, 1987), and a few were in the mainly prose *Life on Limestone* (Smith Settle Ltd, 1994).

Five poems have been broadcast on the 'Poetry Now' programme (BBC Radio 3).

A Paper Ark

This paper boat —
    afloat in Time —
inscribed with runes
    that sometimes rhyme

or sing in tune
    and beat a drum,
would keep undrowned
    till Kingdom Come

the characters
    of beasts and birds
or plants, preserved
    alive in words.

Both Nature's forms
    and that unseen
and nameless one —
    the Go-between

that plucks at chords
    within the heart,
resounding till
    new poems start,

should step aboard
    my folded Ark —
light-weight upon
    the tide of dark —

and navigate
    by mental spark
until the time
    to disembark.

Contents

A Bramley Seedling Apple

Here, sunk in this obese
green apple-belly, sat
the pale five-petalled flower
open to kissing air
that first inflated it.

Behind the apple-bloom
a slender stem
swelled slightly, like the hips
of children, then became
this bulging womb.

Five sepals reach across
the hirsute door
or navel, the same star
that gripped, in tight green claws,
the folded bud, before

its petals yawned, and lured
air's insects, letting in
pollen and maggot, both,
then filled with juicy growth
this taut green skin,

heavy with summer rain,
victim of gravity,
fallen, though still the same
weightless identity
that entered time so lightly.

Ants

Day after day the stony earth, our table,
was cleared by tiny servants. Purple banners
of grapeskin, shreds of yellow velvet peachskin,
were borne out of the shadow where we picnicked,
                          shedding our crumbs of manna.

Then, on our homeward journey, in a layby,
the scooped-out seeds of our last Midi-fruit —
(ten melons for ten francs!) — began to travel
in wavering lines towards the earthen funnel
                          that was Ant-city gate.

At first the walking seeds seemed automobile;
pale yellow forms, far bigger than their porters,
moved hesitantly to the sinking vortex
where struggling ants unlocked the traffic blockage
                          into their Winter quarters.

In metal exoskeletons, the tourists
filter through France, collecting inner postcards:
whole sunflower-fields, small churches, scraps of language,
and swallowtails that, at the touch of shadow,
                          flicker across the vineyards

where ants may still be garnering our litter.
What feasts they carry home: what feasts we carry
through colonnades of planetrees, villages
asleep all afternoon, through forest-tunnels,
                          bearing bright scraps to Calais.

Bat Poem

Bat poems should be written black on black
then black on evening light
when torn triangular wing-writing makes
cursive, quickflickering remarks
along the edge of night.

Ninety percent unseen, mysterious,
they should be a continuous-
ly vanishing surprise,
from pockets of invisibility
materialise
showing anarchic unpredictability
of line-length, disappearing as we stare
into the oval window of the moon,
into thin air.

Illogical, tangential,
they should make sudden dashes after moth
or beetle thoughts
while trawling dusk for truth
or gnats
or both.

They may appear to magnify
moths' orange underwings,
craneflies,
deep ashtree sighs,
distorting fair proportion between things,
for Flittermouse and Noctule's fingerbones
are longer than their thighs.

Bat poems should be silent,
listening,
their gargoyle faces funnelling
the echoes of their own
stuttering decibels
home to the signal drums of Pipistrelles.

For they perceive by hearing:
dancing swarms,
cockchafers, humans loitering alone,
tree-shadows by the lane;
their soundless sound must conjure solid forms
clear on mind's radar screen.

The Bird Garden

The lifers hunch on their perches
waiting for mealtimes, dreaming, remembering
broken promises overheard in the egg,
expectations printed in kidnapped genes
of embryos incubated under lamps
or hatched by fostering bantams in this garden.

Never quite warm enough, the Northern sunlight
shines obliquely, casting long cold shadows.
Peruvians and Amazonians,
a Balinese, and Indian Jungle Fowls —
whose vivid feathers reflect ancestral heat —
wait in their aviaries for life to start.

The great owls doze, but, through insomniac nights,
how can they soar? Seeing the stars through mesh
they imagine forests where they need not hunt,
being deprived of hunger. Through vague days
they yawn, and stretch unnecessary wings —
round-ended, downy feathered, lined for silence.

Two Demoiselles, in dresses out of Vogue,
wear quilly pompoms crowning skull-tight bonnets;
one Demoiselle, being male, opens his wings
to dance a courtship dance; he limps for love,
lightly on spring-hinged legs, because one wing
is pinioned, pruned for his own good.

Rendered flightless to keep them paradise-prisoned,
the crippled dancers pain us with their beauty.
The female spreads her asymmetrical shawl,
hops too high and falls like a hamstrung doll
of walkingsticks and feathers; when risen again
both puppets exit left, to their private limbo.

13

Ducks are a simpler matter. On the lake
the painted Mandarins move like happy toys;
and beauty makes excuses for the theft
of live components out of Nature's process
into this Bird Museum, these prison gardens
where long lives wither slowly as unspent fortunes.

Butterfly Worksong

To be a butterfly is no light matter;

> with glittering rapidity we flutter
> huge sails like airborne windmills, stop the motor

and drill for nectar wells, then, like blown litter,
we putter off again. We are the porters

> in wild art galleries, and shift exhibits
> from dandelions, or thistle-topmost summits,

to gardens in the humans' walled-in quarters.
Each diptych lifts its labouring transporter

> which, inadvertently, in course of duty,
> must pollinate the flowers where, blind to beauty,

we top up fuel tanks of honey-water.
Much put-upon, we batter wings to tatters,

> and if we take time off to understand
> our purposes, the shadow of a hand

destroys our quivering rest. Don't think us flighty;
we dance like sparks to rearrange the weighty

> midsummer exhibition: bear the garden
> on shoulders bowed beneath their gaudy burden

of abstract canvases by the Almighty.

The Necessity for Butterflies

A warthog to a warthog is as pretty
as peacock is to peacock. Painted wings
are hardly necessary to ensure
continuance of species. We appear —
stripped of adopted butterfly attire —
as hairpatched, wingless animals, but lovers
are not thereby struck impotent: far from it.
A raven to a raven is as fair
as hummingbird to hummingbird; the wings
of Swallowtails, in all their variations —
illumination of the world's initials —
express creation's joy in sheer invention.
Hinged chequer-boards, whose patterns have renounced
right-angles and straight lines, whose geometry
has been confused by variable curves,
retain austerity of black and white
and yet these Marbled Whites are not the same
as Magpie Moths or Leopard Moths, or Ermines.
Variety is endless. On this flower
basks a Red Admiral, and on this earth
a sombre wedge splits open and flies off
as a White Admiral, its black and white
embroidered with a few vermilion stitches.
The Common Blue — azure enclosed in speckles —
quarters the ground, seeking a nectar-station,
and finds a dancing-floor of fragrant vetches
where Clouded Yellows, Meadow Browns and Hairstreaks
compete for honey wells. They are not dancing;
this is no waltz to cricket stridulation;
it's less a ballroom than a shopping-centre
where insects purchase nectar. Differing races
are not on speaking terms; from time to time
blue chases yellow, yellow chases brown.
They can't acknowledge beauty not their own.
Yet we find them entrancing, torn-up scraps

of Paradise, with poems for their names
like Purple Emperor and Painted Lady
or Silver-washed Fritillary. We feed
our souls on Camberwell and other beauties
quite useless as a means to any end
that this world understands, but happiness:
gratuitous, unprofitable joy.

Cicadas 1

What are cicadas? Are they a machine
set going by the sun? They sound like one.
With rasps and rifflers, the cicada workers
in cypress factories, demolish silence.
At every edge of its invisible
and seamless tissue, their industrious virtue
is sawing, filing, fraying, drilling holes
till silence is in rags. Where do they live?
They live in the glass houses of their wings
like tiny gargoyles in transparent kennels.
They talk to one another, and they laugh
and laugh, since by sheer force of decibels
their horde subdued the nightingale, and quelled
the butterflies who speak by telephone
in silent languages of pheromones.
What do they live on? Trees: on olive trees
and fruit trees; or on cypresses. I meant
What do they eat? What do you think they eat?
They eat the silence, but for all
their noisy mastication, when night falls
the starry bowl of silence is brim-full.

Cicadas 2

The Summer's claque brings down the house of silence
with hoarse insistent laughter, rattles, uproar;
but when it stops applauding its applause
                    the house of silence stands.
The stars are nailheads in its darkened O.

Mad rookeries of artisans with hacksaws
would fret the tree of silence into toothpicks,
but when their piston elbows rest a moment
                    the tree of silence stands;
they haven't even scored its nameless bark.

Small monumental masons rasp the marble
immensity of silence. They are carving
their own memorial, but files and chisels
                    all fail to mark this stone;
when rifflers stop, the sheer cliff shines, unquarried.

Indifferent to such indifference,
sundriven shifts make Summer's factory
resound with frantic fretwork, and in silence
                    their unseen product stands:
the future, loud with strumming insect bands.

Curlew in July

She walks the wall on bamboo bones
and stands on sentry-duty, and she warns
her children of the holocaust machines.

Once, in the days of scythe and rake,
these meadows were the Kingdom of the Crake.

Now tractors rage all round the field
and mower-blades bite stems, and swathes are felled
to sigh to earth while crouching birds are killed.

The Curlew circles, shrieking panic morse,
returning later to assess her loss.

She voices her shrill queries from the wall,
and shriller pipes respond. Perhaps not all
her chicks, but one plus one, alive and well,

extend their necks to peer above the stubble
like periscopes, but aren't yet out of trouble.

They must survive the siderake and outlast
the deadcart silage-box till it's gone past,
but there are patches where the Corncrake's ghost

still haunts: beside a barn, a knoll too steep
for tractors, and a smear where mud's too deep,

so there Grass Forest stands, and one plus one
may hide while Jackdaws forage on the crown
of Curlew Hill as this day's sun goes down.

If they avoided Undertaker Crow,
at dawn, on fragile legs, the fledglings go

uphill to pastureland. On walltop stones
the mother stalks along on bamboo bones
and splits her beak to utter warning tones

and lullabies and foodcalls, and express
anxiety; her love is half distress
and latent sorrow; such is happiness.

The Dunnock, or Quaker Robin

The robin pacifist, in quaker vest,
   who has renounced war's livery of rage —
the scarlet mask and breast — and quietly dressed
   in grey and brown civilian camouflage,
pleasing to Dunnock taste,

should be a lesson to me, to abjure
   loud strumpet reds and exhibitionist
display of fancy plumage, for demure
   grey feathers; and consider crumbs a feast,
not sparrow-fight for more.

But hear the garden's undemanding guest
   sing "Dunnock eyes see grey as royal blue;
"by robin's bloody bib we're unimpressed;
   "we dance in Dunnock-purple; Dunnocks do
"whatever they like best.

"Our coloured glassbead eyes illuminate
   "our own grey kind with lovelight. Dunnock lust
"is roused by Dunnocks, and our appetite
   "is for such morsels Dunnocks can digest,
"and more is out of sight."

Chinese Geese

We summoned emperors to clip the croft
and are abashed. With heads aloft,
our gardeners bring beauty as a gift.

Utility serves whom? Useful to what?
Is beauty functional, or not?
Disdainfully they strut

in milky-coffee-coloured uniform,
with warm nape-stripe, and fine white-ribbon line
seeming to bind on extra brain

or sealed third eyes, but cartilage, in fact.
The male wears larger pseudo-intellect,
drinks first, and walks in front. Both walk erect,

keep close together, seem to share one mind,
and look, from orange-outlined eyes,
askance at humankind.

Do we seem beautiful to geese?
We have a certain water-bearing use,
and frighten foxes. Goosebill scissors grass,

serving goose-appetite, and us; but what
is usefulness in aid of, but god's art?
On orange feet goose-mandarins step out.

April Thoughts of a Broody Goose

Slowly, slowly, the sun goes broody
warming her sullen egg, and turning
white to brown, and lighting brown with
                         emeralds burning.

Gently she hatches buds, and gently
coaxes, from bald brown mud, green freckles;
mottles the cherrytree's birth-bloodied bosom —
                      thrushlike with speckles.

Closer, the sky-goose settles, closer.
I grow heavy with ganderfruits:
(dipping, we drank, he gripped my nape,
his webbed feet trod my pinion roots;

rump to white rump we kissed, and called
the goosegods down; light entered me:)
these faceless stones are gosling-pods —
                      ignorantly, I see.

Daylong, nightlong, I am possessed
by sunlike love. I must warm each world
where, in underdown nest, goose-past
                      filters futureward, seamlessly sealed.

Widow Goose

O comfort her with apples
    and comfort her with bread,
for now she eats and sleeps alone
    upon her table-bed.

She clips the tufted table-cloth:
    her gander's counterpane;
he lost his footing on the earth,
    fell headfirst in the drain.

So comfort her with apples
    and comfort her with bread;
he lies with all his plumage on,
    beneath her table bed.

Though he was an infanticide
    who killed each gosling child
that crept from underneath his bride,
    to her his heart was mild.

So comfort her with apples
    for, though she's lost her mate,
and he his sweet and only life,
    she's kept her appetite.

He was her faithful shadow
    until his sun went down;
together on our meadow
    they strolled and preened as one.

But give her bread and apples,
    and a far better thing —
a bridegroom, a new gander
    to tread her in the Spring.

The Death of Our Goose

She disappeared in the dark;
   she disappeared in clouded midwinter weather
between brief day and day,
   leaving no trace of a fight, neither blood nor feather:
                so we go home to silence.

The darkness swallowed her whole:
   a starless night had bagged her in its wallet;
between dim dusk and dawn
   the moonless midnight gulped her down its gullet;
                so we go home to silence.

A dog turned wolf, or a fox,
   or some other sharp-toothed agent, under cover
of midnight's muffled clocks
   has snatched her; she is at one with her buried lover,
                and we go home to silence.

Her Gander was her fortress
   and sentinel; he fenced her round with fierce
display, both night and day,
   and lacking him she was made sacrifice.
                So we go home to silence.

Digested by the dark,
   she lurks in the early shadows, or flaps with rooks —
at close of winter days —
   home to the black-barred copse or the cleft in the rocks
                as we go home to silence.

Dispersed, and no longer alone,
   she has enlisted in night's legions, left
the light of widowed days,
   bequeathing us her absence. Our house is bereft,
                and we go home to silence.

Goat Music

Across the mountain river, whose white boulders —
huge washed potatoes — shoulder swift green waters,
a wooded rampart rises into shadow.
Young chestnut-trees step down old terraces
right to the current's margin, so the forest
dabbles its fringes, paddles its bare roots
in snow-today-and-sea-tomorrow torrents.
Beyond the water-babble, a metallic
random tune emerges from the greenwood
and, growing louder, puts in an appearance.
Spontaneous music is being written down
left-handedly, along a stave of footpaths
running beside the river, horizontal
to bar-line treeboles, by a ringing rabble
of goats, some sheep like breves, one gracenote dog.
They clank, then hesitate; they nibble leaves
then, singly or as chords, move on
to improvise haphazard phrases, plucking
slack strings of wavering paths.
Some goats are dark as crotchets, others brown,
khaki or creamy-white; these varying tones
and colours might imply the various pitches
of hammered goat-bells, but no calculation
comes into it. The goats compose, write in
and then erase their one
never-to-be-repeated daily tune.
The last notes loiter, wait for their conductor
and exit left, though — pianissimo —
a far off scherzo crosses the main road
towards the goat-sheds; then I hear again
the irreversibly continuous song
of water and the woodwinds of the trees.

Brother Fox

Men net the seeming-docile hills
    in mesh of walls, but fail
to kill the fox of the high fells
    who lives beyond the pale.

I trickle under drystone walls
    while staid law-keepers dream,
and creep, when mooncast shadow falls,
    towards the valley farm.

The serpent writhes in my backbone,
    the snake dances in yours,
and treacherously lets me in
    to snap my wanton jaws.

Men load the valley fields with walls
    but still cannot subdue
the bandit of the stony fells
    who lives, deep-earthed, in you.

I trot, blood-dark, close by the wall
    under snow-smothered moon,
printing bad news with each footfall
    towards the winking town.

The serpent writhes in my backbone,
    the snake dances in yours,
and hypnotises gentlemen
    into bloodlust and wars.

Five Serious Limericks

in homage to Gilbert White of Selborne

The reverend naturalist
is dumb on Jehovah and Christ:
   reads lessons on swallows
   and martins, their fellows,
for the Joker is known by his jest.

In letters and notebooks he makes
observations and seldom mistakes;
   sees preaching to birds
   to be sheer waste of words
so listens to curlews and crakes.

Obsessed by a thought that revolves,
Gilbert White never finally solves
   whether swallows migrate
   or remain, hibernate
or depart. Slowly knowledge evolves.

The Parson of Selborne's keen eyes
spotted no lurking God-in-disguise
   nor Angels alight:
   the devout Gilbert White
saw them larking about in the skies,

and the swift, fast asleep in midair,
that circles the tower top where
   his mate keeps her station
   of nidification
was deity, hymnbook and prayer.

The Carpet-Slippered Hare

Dotted and dashed, the indiscreet
    snow broadsheet tells the news
in morse tapped out by long back feet
    and ladylike front paws;
"The carpet-slippered hare grows desperate
    for straws."

Gnawing our cabbage to its root,
    (dropped pellets pay the bill),
he hobbles off, no longer fleet,
    finds nothing left to fill
his belly, levers himself — hunger-light —
    uphill.

While proley rabbits crowd in holes,
    aloof but down-and-out
Hare sits on fitted carpet soles
    for comfort. Delicate
front paws scratch snow for grass, but blizzard seals
    his fate.

Hissing and whispering, the sleet —
    past flattened ears, dim eyes —
flies horizontal, cakes his coat,
    but ice lacks calories;
so Hare falls off his ill-assorted feet
    and dies.

Laughing, the undertaker crows
    dismember him, and eat;
but on the piebald hill grass grows
    more green as snows retreat.
There, cantering on well-heeled slipper-toes,
    Hares meet.

The Freeholder

A small brown alien from space
   arrived on our acre
   as naked as his maker
first finished him, and he surveyed the place.

With sideways eyes in a blunt face
   and upright ears that swivelled round,
   he cased our ground;
then stretched up tall as tallest grass

to nip a seed-head from its stem
   and chew it well and swallow
   the sweet wild bread. This fellow
knew what was good for him.

He washed, with neat front feet,
   his furry cheeks, then hopped
   to eat some more, then stopped;
sat on his country seat.

He was so much at home,
   at ease in his brown skin,
   I realised our bought domain
by rights belonged to him.

Though he dropped in on me
   and honoured me with trust,
   I was the interloping guest
of Hare the refugee.

Ivy Leaved Toadflax

Yes, I admit to being
opportunistic, clinging —
    because I lack all rights —
    to intersticial sites.

Stones, desert-dry and bald,
allow me fingerhold;
    fingers and toes take root
    and fix my fragile net

of mini-ivy leaves
on climbing stems. I weave
    small hanging gardens, light
    as cobwebs, almost, out

of stoneground crumbs of mortar
and drops of holy water
    till toothless dragon faces
    blossom in arid places.

You may wish I adorned
your dwelling, but be warned:
    I will not be transplanted
    to grow where I am wanted.

Mysteriously, my seed
finds lodgement. I am weed
    or nothing. Post and lintel
    cannot command my mantle.

I seem autonomous,
and yet I do not choose
    but grow where I am sent,
    being obedient

to codes broadcast through time
out of the One-Word Tome.
    Genomes determine all;
    my will accepts its wall.

To the Finger-Footed Ringtailed Lemur

Prosimian, grand-ancestor of Man,
contributor of uniformity —
grey suit, white mask, long underwear and scarf —
out of the Malagasey trees to us
                    in our complexity.

Always correctly dressed, club-membership
is written in your genes, so mavericks
must be unthinkable. Exchanging passwords,
you keep together and reject outsiders
                    and eccentricity.

You share one consciousness and dream one dream
sleeping in cliques bound by the old school tail —
long black-and-white ringed boas, intertwined —
until one flea bites all, and orange eyes
                    wake simultaneously

to stare through regulation spectacles.
Your make-up won't wash off, your joke-shop teeth
are real, and old men's combinations hide
nothing; you wear your genitals outside,
                    even in company.

Though thought is free, you think in unison
and, worshipping one god, expose
your vulnerable bellies and the white
inside of tender arms, embracing light
                    from forest canopy.

Each day is Sunday. Like a soul on heat
for god, you woo his light-rays, then embrace
your fellows without guile. Question-mark tails
answer themselves, and get the answer right
                    in wise simplicity.

A Lobster for John Milton

If, like a crab, I could go back
three centuries, I would in eloquent
and latinate Miltonic verse declaim
that I the scuttling seabed crab observe
to bear his body-head, or offal pie,
sideways on spider legs, brandishing pairs
of pincer thumbs on swollen elbows, while
backward from danger lobsters leap, propelled
by fanning, bright blue tails. This insect large
and submarine, that gnashes the false teeth
it holds in hornier hands than ever yet
mechanic used, the spanner, pliers or wrench
to wield, (they more resemble tools than hands),
moves often in reverse, with parts misplaced.
Eyes swivel lidless, but his tail fan-plates
with eyelashes of golden silk are fringed,
and tenderly the female lobster bears
her spawn, not in her arms, but pseudopods
close underneath her pliant-armoured tail.
Her arms are power-driven knives and forks,
and not for love's embraces. Genial play
through scarlet aerials of tapering
nerve-threaded beads, is feelingly expressed
when Lobster dances on eight bone-skinned limbs
and joyful rite of mating celebrates.
Strangely, to me, these monsters justify —
by ultramarine blue, deep seaweed-red
and white-bossed beauty, God's creative play.
Machines for living — tenant, house and car —
fit for their purpose, to exist, they know
no doubt; are unforsaken even when
face first into the boiling cauldron flung.

Great Mullein

First seen on Inishmore,
   your green pagodas grew
   man-high across the limestone plain
by the Kilmory shore.

Clothed in decurrent tongues
   that cling and wrap you up
   in lapping leaves, your stem withstands
the force of weeping winds.

I sent some stolen seeds
   home to my father's house;
   he grew, by his suburban door,
some proud defiant weeds.

He's ash these thirty years
   of troubles, tides and stars;
   now I've achieved a colony
of velvet volunteers.

Erect, leaf-buttressed towers —
   mossed grey with woolly down —
   stretch visibly, in warm July,
to steeplejacking flowers.

Each bud, close packed in hair,
   towards its tower-top
   opens a sulphur-yellow shop
for customers of air

and sells the hoverfly
   sweet fuel for energy;
   it asks, in fee, brief bliss
and continuity.

Magpies

One's for sorrow; two appear for joy
to glitter along the edge of a threadbare wood
and overlook the scavenging riffraff rooks
and sober, industrious jackdaws that walk the field
prodding the mud for food.

More like enormous tropical butterflies
than British birds, they are crows that have won the pools
and wear evening dress all day, so, with springy strut,
they show off satin shirts, white epaulettes,
and iridescent, green and blue silk tails.

With flashy wings they flutter, freewheel, flap,
seem casual, but loiter with intent;
through spyholes in black hoods they case the joint —
this green upholstered landscape — preen and scratch
and wait for singing chickens' eggs to hatch.

Fine feathers make fine crows — mere liar birds —
both lucky and unlucky, like the rest.
Perhaps some gamekeeper could not resist
the target of those guiltless villains' vests;
or have they flown to roost in taller trees

with better views, and built a bonfire nest
such as success deserves? For I have missed
my first and second murderers for days:
now hear them shake their bones, deep in the woods;
haunting, immortal in their shot-silk shrouds.

The Party

The lamp in our rented room
beams out across the gardens
making an autoroute of light
in open invitation to the moths
and all the Midi's strange nocturnal flies.
We cannot have the cool night air
without such visitors, and is it worse
to suffocate in stuffiness
or welcome in this random throng?
We opt for air and hospitality.
By August all the insect tribes have grown
innumerable, various and bold.
Our guests come dressed to kill,
cloaked in minute invisibility
or armoured like machines —
as airborne tanks or zeppelins —
to raid our undefended space.
The landlady's faded wallpaper
develops a pattern of moths,
but these are amiable enough
and some are beautifully dressed
in soft-fringed, grey old ladies' shawls:
their folded wings.
But smaller brutes, the whining kind,
creep furtively up sleeves or skirts
to syphon out our blood.
If they dare pierce my husband's pelt
he swats them promptly, or goes hunting,
dancing about the room and shouting *Got you!*
clapping his hands on nothing.
I've trained myself in politeness far too well.
I sometimes think I have an Alcestis complex.
If all these vampires did was take a drink
I wouldn't mind at all, they would be welcome.
Female mosquitoes need such food
to nourish unborn young, and who am I

to grudge the sacred rights of Motherhood?
But where their drinking-straws have been
they leave a poison residue
so, all next day, and for days to come,
I wear a spotted skin.
I crave to scratch, control myself,
then suddenly go frantic and draw blood.
These irritations are a part of Summer.
Air couldn't feed the swallows or the bats
without her swarms of microdots,
and hosts must tolerate some biting flies
or shut their doors.

The Rat-Tailed Maggot (Drone-fly Larva)

This larva in his pool
does not enquire
if he is beautiful or foul,
Lord Mayor or pariah;
but, in the bottom layer
of creatures, is content
to feed on cess-pit slime
while breathing in fresh air
through his extended tail
that reaches through the scum
that lids his home.

He feels no shame or guilt,
is not disgusted with
his status in the scheme
of nature: "Useful tool,
even a holy fool,
is what I am, I am,"
he murmurs as he sweeps —
with bristles round his lips —
the silt into his gob;
while at the distant tip
of his long breathing-tube
two tiny spiracles
imbibe the oxygen
that hints at miracle:
that there is light and air
somewhere up there.

"I am, I am, I am;"
he murmurs as he creeps
about until his youth
is spent, and then he sleeps;
and in his sleep he sings
about the sunlit world
where he has wings.

A Salamander Song

for Ken Livingstone

My mother was a humble axolotl,
    as was my father; I was not brought up
to be a Salamander but a glottal-
    stopping larval form: an axolotl pup.

For axolotls are the lower orders;
    they live and breed as tadpoles in their lake;
dry land is hot and horrid round its borders,
    to step ashore and leave is a mistake.

A Salamander's chocolate skin is patterned
    with ocelotty spots, while axolotls —
blunt-muzzled, with tails laterally flattened —
    are grey as embryos in pickle-bottles.

Yet axolotls take their simple pleasures;
    their faces may be shapeless as old boots,
but they desire and mate; they spawn live treasures;
    I don't despise my axolotl roots.

The restless and excitable try harder
    to undergo a metamorphosis;
a constant food supply, the well-stocked larder,
    makes them phlegmatic and inhibits this,

but in the stimulating air of Paris
    in eighteen-sixty-five, so history tells,
some axolotl tadpoles did not tarry
    in water but emerged and shed their gills,

and thus men learned that the submerged, aquatic
    proteidae, with opportunity,
could turn to beautiful, meritocratic,
    terrestrial Salamanders, fine as me.

I am an object-lesson in the case
    for education of all sons and daughters
of the exploited axolotl race
    who rise out of the amniotic waters.

A Sun King with Earth Queens

The metallic cough of the coppery King-in-exile
heralds the pheasants' arrival, requests our attention
although he has nothing to say but "Look at me, look
at the burnished scales of my soft, ceremonial armour,
the springy plumes of my cantilevered tail
and gold-buttoned armistice poppies on either cheek;
observe my priestly collar and seagreen cowl
but do not notice my modestly camouflaged Queens."

During our absence, one morning, he dropped us a feather;
its chestnut filaments had been dipped in sunlight
though, near its root, it was grey with thermal down.
This gold-tipped message informed us that he had called.
Twice daily he ushers his shy harem through our weeds;
his seven furtive princesses in brownspeckled tweeds
consider that ours is a safe house. Increasingly silent,
we bang few doors and fail to mow our lawns.

Perched on the topmost rail of our shaky fence,
the resplendent King proclaims a palace-garden
of coltsfoot beds, and hedges spread into thickets;
his dowdy Queens nod automatic approval,
pecking at mosses between wild raspberry canes.
If I go out with the washing, I beg their pardon,
conceding squatters' rights to the Wilderness,
and title deeds to the Royal Concubines.

Dappled with sunspots, deep in the undergrowth,
they crouch, disguised as shadows or drifts of leaves,
and brood over crucibles full of the Royal Genes.
The gilded King steps out and coughs, midfield,
to draw the fire of our attention: "Look
at my eldorado armour, my glaring eyes
buttoning blood-petalled poppies for brothers you killed;
my Queens are restoring the dead in their time-machines."

The White Pheasant

after Chernobyl

Like the morning mountain, grizzled white
as though some dreadful news on the northwest gale
had turned it grey overnight,

an ashen pheasant haunts this greening dale.
Perhaps last Summer's penetrating rain
has bleached it in the egg. A milky veil —

like cloud that hides and then betrays the moon —
lies on its roof of plumage: cape and crest,
wing-coverts, pinions, rump and tapered train.

Its tower neck is navy-blue, its breast
a dried-blood red, but, surpliced in soiled snow,
it walks aloof and chaste.

His conker-coloured cocketting brother crows
and struts before a prosy brown harem;
the sunrise kindles him until he glows

rose-red, and catches fire; his feathers flame
and dazzle the assenting hens. He shakes
sparks from his wings, and shouts his common name

again. But, circumspectly, through the brake,
steps the frosted pheasant, bearing runes
in dark calligraphy on its pale cloak.

We cannot read these loops and scrolls, these lines
of penmanship's fine pot-hooks, but we guess
the letters warn. The living letter warns.

But beauty proves to be Cassandra's curse.
No-one believes. Spring bears the usual gifts
of budding leaves and birdsong, none the worse.

The bird stalks uphill to the copse that sifts
bright beads from mist. It couches all alone
in sedge among the stained and dwindling drifts

and knows itself as sterile as the moon.

The Rams

Our croft is now an athenaeum of rams
whose testicles are bigger than their brains,
or so it would appear; hot bottles swing
between high-heeled back legs, air-cooled,
while, at the other end, their skulls
consist of Roman nose and G.I. jaws.
Above their spaced-out, golden-alley eyes
they have no brows to speak of, and whereof
we cannot speak thereof we should keep silent,
as they do in our lime-tree's tent of shade.

They congregate like mute philosophers
to ruminate on August aftergrass
which must improve their spermcount with each mouthful.
That is what they are here for. In October
they'll have to ramrod every germen home.
Meanwhile they rest in judgelike gravity
upon an edible green carpet-pile
while magpie waiters dance attendance on them,
bouncing across the turf onto their flanks
to pick the parasites from dreadlock wigs.

The new-made swifts try out long-distance wings,
racing between woolgatherings of cloud
dyed pink by sunset, as is August's first
half-moon to southward. Furtive thrushes steal
our rowanberries, and dismantle Summer.
Meanwhile, boneheaded but wiseblooded augurs
conserve their strength, conceiving prophecies
of Springtime in their baggage. They foresee
next April through potential eyes of lambs
pendent between their dung-encrusted limbs.

The Hospitality of Rowan Trees

The summer-long slow burn of mountain ashes
prepares a feast. Light blossom-froth was starters,
but the main course, dragging the pliant twigs
earthward with heaviness, is berry-clusters
cooked to come-hither scarlet. Guests arrive.
Pot-shaped wood pigeons agitate the leaves
with flutterings and gluttony, and blackbirds
tabletalk and food-call, sotto voce,
while balancing on lithe unstable perches
and picking fruit precisely, with neat beaks.
They eat for weeks but do not strip the tree.
The starling squadrons do that in one day.
Gatecrashers spread the word, and avid flocks
pour out of nowhere, fill the tree with wings
and put an end to hospitality.

The festive baubles, painted by the sunlight
with many coats of colour as they grew:
green, brown, tan, orange, deeper orange, scarlet;
all luminous with warm ingested rays,
are lost, the feast for human eyes reduced
to tired and dowdy salad of green leaves.
This was not rape or theft but deed of gift;
not altruism either, but exchange.
The Rowan casts its bread upon the air —
red pellets gulped by gullets, crushed in crops —
in reciprocity. The tree provides
wages for seed-dispersing foresters
who feed and scatter future Rowan trees.
Losing its life to save it, nature gives;
the principle is generosity.

Common Starlings

About the layered air,
    like locusts, starling-kind
wheel in great flocks above the city square:
    quite leaderless, and yet so disciplined
    they seem to share one mind.

Even the dreaming seer
    remembered starling-kind
as numerous and nameless, in his Hell;
    he saw their dustclouds whirling in the wind
    of lust, borne round and round.

My earth-besotted eyes
    and Dante's are combined
in wonderment at many forming one
    when, instant as the louvres of a blind,
    the birds, to no command,

turn, flashing in the sun.
    Sound instinct is the wind
their undiminished numbers ride through time;
    lust orders doubtful reason jettisoned;
    impulse and act are joined.

Angelic privates drill
    for bloodless wars, descend
by corporate and democratic will,
    fill leaftiled sycamores with squealing sound,
    survey their feeding-ground,

then raid our rowantree
    whose burdened boughs extend
bloodscarlet berry clusters, offered free
    to chatterers and flutterers who lend
    excited twigs, at Summer's end,

brief foliage of wings.

A Riddle, with Answer

These hairy strangers see by night
or daylight through their six or eight
eye-portholes round their brainy part.

No necks: their head and chests are one;
and they are nimble-fingered on
four pairs of seven-jointed limbs

that climb and run, dance minuets,
crochet rose-windowframes, glass nets,
footworking silk from spinnerets.

Ingenious light engineers,
they rise on fraying gossamers
to travel upper atmospheres

with swarms of parachuting seeds,
plankton of current-carried weeds
on flying insects' random roads.

Yes, they are small, these aliens,
so, though they're fierce, with poison fangs
like penknives, they don't bother Man

who welcomes in age-old outsiders:
trapeze artistes, high-wire hang-gliders
in pearly tents. We call them Spiders.

The Silver Spider

i.m. C. von Wyss

I found her in a book —
    my latest pet —
and keep her in a pond —
    deep, dark and wet —
    inside my thinking-nut.
So look, please look
at my aquatic friend
among the water-fronds.

She was not pressed out flat,
    trapped in that tome,
but free to swim and dive
    to her own home —
    an underwater dome —
through clear descriptions that
preserve alive
all things the writer loves.

Among the pondweed groves
    my silver pet —
who wears a vest of air
    and hangs a level net
    from water-violet
or other pondweed leaves —
survives undrowned down there
in her silkwoven lair

by furnishing her home
    with airy spheres
entrapped and carried down
    in body hairs
    so the wee beast appears
silver. She fills her dome
with brushed-off bubble gowns
that hid her greys and browns.

Her husband weaves his den
    beside her house
and lives in his own space:
    a lucky spouse
    among the spider race
of cannibals: amen.
Avoiding murderous disgrace,
they live in peace.

So I must praise their kind,
    also the one
who watched, and wrote a book
    about the submarine
    arachnid, then
passed on, from mind to mind,
her wonder, let us look
at Spiders' life and work.

Wolf-Spider's Song to her Young

for John Clare, who described this creature so well

Baglady-like, a vagabond,
    I carry you, my precious eggs,
parcelled in silk beneath my round
    fat belly in a cage of legs.

I am your cradle and your car,
    and when you hatch to spiderlings
I am your warhorse — life is war —
    cling to my mane, small riderlings.

At danger's touch you scatter, hide
    till threats are past, then take your seat:
climb on, hold tight, away we ride
    lassooing grasshoppers to eat.

All Summer long, in clover-groves,
    we lurk, and pounce, then feast. You grow
till shorter days decree, my loves,
    that you spin gossamers and go.

The Autumn winds waft you away
    so high, so far, to some new world;
and left alone, grown old and grey,
    I shrivel in the frosty field.

Wolf-Spider's Cradle Song

I am your cradle and your pram,
   sleep sweetly, little eggs;
I am your chariot, your tram,
   I roll on well-sprung legs.

I am your rocking cradle-ship
   to cross the ploughland main;
I'll take you on a long sea trip
   and bring you home again.

And when you open your eight eyes
   I'll be your minibus:
the shining spiders of the skies
   look kindly down on us.

I am your cradle and your pram,
your ship, your minibus, your tram
   but cannot be your jumbo-jet
   so operate each spinneret;
    invent yourself a parachute.
Farewell, good luck, from Mam.

The Snails

All night, into my sleep, a whispering
insinuated images of rain
falling on thirsty leaves. Its crystal drops
spiralled round hostas' dishy parasols
to find the open downspout to the root.

At morning I discovered my small garden
transformed into a succulent green salad
for large, well-lubricated snails that quested —
with phallic necks extended, horns erect
and crowned with tiny eyeballs — over pasture.

They were so large, so many, so voracious;
I pulled some off my foxgloves and my hostas —
though frilled feet kissed and clung — and then I tossed them
over the fence into the unseen weeds
of my eccentric neighbour. Then desisted.

Eager explorers of their verdant world,
with lower horns tap-tapping like white sticks,
they had emerged from dry brick crevices
and stacks of flowerpots to celebrate
this rainy rave-in. Soon the birds would get them.

Where is the thrushes' golgotha for snails?
and Blackbird, hooded executioner?
My snails graze unmolested, meet and mate —
linked by a glistening hawser of white flesh —
each one the centre of their shared green world,

exchanging fluids in a mess of mucus.
At dusk I find a demolition gang
of brittle-turbanned molluscs on the tiles
of my blue hosta-temple, stripping it,
while sad pagoda foxgloves stand in rags.

Another night's conspiratorial rain
makes lace of my green farm:
its hospitality's destroyed by guests —
leaf-mincers with no hearts — while I recoil
from crushing underfoot this crowd of beasts.

The Sunflowers

With laiking southerners' extravagance
   I sowed this northern hill with sunflowerseed,
though sighing ash and thorn might scorn the dance
   of heliotropic-tilting leaf and head.

I shivered in my exile, (Spring delayed),
   and longed to grow tall vegetable suns,
an infant god's flame bonnet, self-portrayed:
   a troupe of haloed clowns.

Devotedly I watered, through May's drought,
   twin cotyledons, cunningly tugged out
of splitting husks, to balance on one foot
   and juggle with the light.

They drank, through June, the grey incessant rain
   and fed their cordate rags on cold and wet;
by twos and threes, leaves clambered toward noon
   long after noon, and no bloom budded yet.

None flowered when September gales laid waste;
   reclined, oblique, my solar totems lay:
but each raised a defiant, green-clawed fist,
   and each fist held an eye.

These spiky hands were heads, and all their minds
   were compound lenses, wrapped in eyelash fringe,
till straight through Winter's ruined borderlands
   a south wind breathed on each stiff petal-hinge.

Slowly they splash the dusk with wheels of flame
   to bear me through the dark; grave offerings:
coronas of eclipse, at curfew time:
   the tattered paper crowns of beggar kings.

Swift Season

Scattered cohorts of innocent bees
rummage the frothy meadowsweet plumes,
searching, searching for fugitive treasure,
packing their whiskery thighs with gold.

Rising and falling like fur-bellied crotchets,
they hum the bass that underlines
the shriller-than-treble hooligan choir
of distant screamers overhead

panicking me into consciousness
of Summer's flight, which is swifter than swifts
that circle the sky in excited swarms
of high soprano topnotes, being

international primadonnas
in midsummer's opera. From the wings
I hear the flypast of too many summers
whirring away and vanishing.

Few can be left. The meadowsweet fades
and tarnishes to sober seed, as
fledgling swifts perfect their flight
on long dark blades, before they leave,

while something within me stands and grieves
for migrant years. I am possessed
by dread of winter and being dead:
timelust, not to be satisfied.

Tortoiseshells Overwintering

In my bedroom ceiling's shadiest corner
   a dark encampment of inverted tents
is sitting out the tyranny of Winter.

Like Israelites that keep God's covenants
   in sober arks, or nomad Bedouins
who hide rich mats in fustian tenements,

they fold the magic carpets of their wings,
   concealing hieroglyphics of the meadow
clapped between tatter-bordered coverings.

As dingy as the withered nettlebed,
   as drab as marbled bibles, charred by fire,
or chips of bark or stone, they could be dead

but hang by wiry legs, as fine as hair,
   close-clustered near the plaster desert's edge
like a proscribed religious sect at prayer.

This bivouac preserves the Summer's page
   during eclipse of dandelions and daisies;
it bears pressed sparks of sun through this dark age: —

one night between oasis and oasis.

Wasps' Nest

Beneath our lintel hung a papery breast
nippled with penetrating dark that pierced
the layered curtain of the queen wasp's nest.

Out of this Summer palace, princelings flew;
some hunted, some had building work to do;
the population and the palace grew.

They fetched new woodpulp, added paper ridges
and, working backwards along selvages,
turbanned the nest in mummy bandages.

A cabbage with grey leaves, drilled by a worm:
a pendent dome: a tumour on the beam:
a paper brain that hummed with thoughts of home:

The prison chapel of a pregnant nun
who crouched in prayer, walled up from the sun,
to bear her thousand children, one by one.

Her nursery, inverted tree of pods,
has hatched its hundreds, but the queen still adds
more eggs, possessed by Summer's dying gods.

The princes' number dwindles. Still tight-laced
and elegant as ever — isthmus waist
links tiger bustle to her pigeon chest —

the venerable queen within the walls
sits brooding over trays of cradle cells
where perfect wasps lie dead beneath their seals.

A secret monument to Summer past,
she dessicates in darkness, grey with dust,
killed by the silent treachery of frost.

Wren-Sermon, or Smallest is Sacred

The flightless bipeds, ponderously slow
as insubstantial trolls of cumulus
that loll about the table of the world,
emerge from house to garden, come and go
    while I, as quick as blinking, quick as light,
    dart out of sight.

Obtuse beyond belief, they think I am
    a flying leaf, a shadow, russet rag,
    a mouse run to its crevice in the crag
which shelters me among the armoured game
    that scuttles, quick as winking, quick as light,
    out of my sight.

Quicker than I, the summer hoverfly
    changes its airy stations. Glassy wings
    sustain, invisibly, its humming stance
until it shifts, quite unpredictably,
    to hang a foot away, as quick as shot,
    first here, then not.

The frantic gnats must think it vast and slow,
    but are themselves composed of energies
    like instantaneous eternities:
light particles that shuttle to and fro
    as quick as inspiration, cheating thought,
    setting the table out.

Warning to a Worm

An alimentary tract
   undressed in flesh and bone
   should not be out alone;
that's elementary fact.

Go home, small hoover-pipe:
   go home, elastic hose
   that lacks a leg, that grows
and then contracts its shape;

Segmented, tapered tube:
   twin-ended tentacle:
   go home, small article
of food, before birds grab

and eat you. Hurry. Rush.
Beware the savage Thrush.

Zoo Pelicans

Schoolboys answer the reproachful stare
of the rare Dalmatian Pelican with jests:
"Dodo-bird," one calls it, "Dodo-bird."
With eyes like pale blue marbles, maestro hair,
begonia-leaflike feet, and reticule
slung from the flexible rami of its bill,
it speaks no word so cannot make mistakes
unlike the Parents telling Innocents
"They're Swans:" "They're ugly funny ones:" "They're Storks:"
seeing Creation as a hall of mirrors
where creatures fail at being like themselves.

The Pelicans turn their handbags inside-out,
yawning and dreaming of buoyant unpinioned flight
or fishing in wavering lines across wide bays.
Whimpering Gulls are privileged beggars who snatch
and fly when Keeper brings the already-dead fish
in a plastic bucket, and flings it. Pelicans catch,
or miss and dip for it, filling elastic chins,
like swollen udders, with water that filters away,
leaving the fish to be swallowed. Five minutes a day
of frantic dashing and gulping compensate
for the loss of the communal hunt of the Lords of the Shore.

Yet even these prisoners on this pond are grand
as fully-rigged galleons, silver and snowy, black-flagged
and paddling-legged, propelled towards the land
where Pelicans preen and confer, leave no feather unturned
or undressed with oil from the codliver-brylcreem gland.
Each fishbucket beak is also a one-toothed comb
and feathery napes are clothesbrushes, grooming each cape.
Every bird is its own busy barber's shop,
and each is a mystery, tall as a ten-year-old child,
made in the shape of the Pelican Maker, and filled
with the Mythical Pelicans' reedbed and watery world.